Encyclopedia of Decoding Sleep.

How the Brain Deals With Sleep.

DAVID GOMADZA

PAPERBACK ISBN: 9798323320868:

DEDICATION

To a better future.

CONTENTS

1 How the Brain Deals With Sleep. 1

ACKNOWLEDGMENTS

To Tomorrow's World Order

How the Brain Deals With Sleep.

Closeyoureyes
Startbinaryrecoveryplanxt
Start.endallprocesses.start
Start.when.start
Startifidontsleepthenwhat.start
Ifidontsleep.start
Ifidosleepdreamswhichones.start
Ifidreamwhichdreams.save
Now look up in the sky and say I want to sleep
What happens
Close curtains of the soul and sleep
Sleep.start.now
Whenyousleepaskwhatif.start
Ifyousleepaskwhy.start
Ifiaskwhy.start
Then start
Now see if you sleep you will literally sleep flat first yen deep sleep
Now if we Ask what to do when we sleep this is the reply pray you dream about a wife
Now let's look at the codes that put you in a trance
Ifisleepdoaskaboutdreams.start
Wheniclosemyeyesstart.ask
Wheniaskadreamwhichone.start
Wheniaskyouyourdream.start
Whenisaysleep.start

Whenisleep.start
Wheniwakeup.start
Ifidontwakeupthen.start
Ifiaskwhatis.start
Whenlask.start
Whenwas.start
Whencouldtherebe.start
Onsleep.stop
Dontstop.start
Dontstart.sleep
Don'tsleep.start
Whenistart.sleep
Whenistart.sleep
Whenisleep.start
Whendontstart.sleep.start
When.start.sleep
When.sleep.disturb.now
When.sleep.start.nowactive.start
When.start.sleep.is.not.mine.start
Whenisleepaskhow.start
Whenisleep.start.now
Whenisleep.thenaskhow.now.start
Ifidontsleep.start
Ifidontsleep.start.youcanstart.now.start
Ifisleepthenwakeupdontsleepagainfor20minutes.start.thensleep.start
Whenisleep.now.ask.whatif.start
Whenisleep.ok.start
Whenisleep.start.ifyoucanaskwhatwoulditbe.start
Whenisleep.now.whotoask.start.now.start
Whenisleep.dream.start
Whenidream.start
Whendreaming.start
Whendreamingamplify.imageforgreatexperiences.start
Ifisleep.start.ask.what.anythingnice.start
Ifisleepaskwhatcanbedone.start
Don't ask.whatif.start.insleep.start
Dontaskwhatcanbedone.start
Dontaskwhatistobedone.start
Dontasktalkinsleep.start

Donttalkbutactionspeechinsleep.start
Dontaskbutlisten.start
Dontstart.starttofinish
Ifiaskthenlisten.start [acetate talking back to you in sleep everyone apart me]
I can tell the world that Yahweh him and the other 3 take turns to sleep but they can and are full aware of actual events
Let's look at dreams in the creator Yahweh
Yahweh take turns to guard himself as well with the help of the others namely
Catitighit Joseph and Anna all of them don't have auditorium grand chamber instead they have auditorium conference room this is what makes Yahweh not sleep but quench sleep just like humans who do sleep
If we Ask how this is possible this is the answer Yahweh is a powerful God who attracts powerful enemies and as such who ever created Yahweh created him with divine safety in mind in that Yahweh since they are all joined all cannot sleep like humans what they do is to exchange sleeping points during day these points are like rights to sleep if you own these that means you will automatically knockout someone until your sleep is quenched then the next must do the same to the next one in Yahweh this complexity somehow which is strange comes with predefined parameters which is suspicious because
this points to someone above Yahweh quick question is there someone above Yahweh?
Yahweh insists no one is above him but today I found who is above Now I will tell you how I found out I removed human limitations and capabilities and discovered that human limitations are there to block us asking further questions Yahweh is assigned to look after humans as a God hence since you are all humans you mist know only about Yahweh but say turn me into another creature I turn myself to a lion

Now let's see the codes involved in such a setting
If we are to ask what.if this is the answer you can't challenge Yahweh let alone Yahweh's creator
You can ask what.if yourself
No reply

Now let's continue with the question at hand if sleep don't come then what to do
1] askwhy.start
2] askwhen.start.start
3] ask.whatif.start
4] ask.start
5] ask.when.start
6] ask.how.start
7] ask.why.now
8] ask.whatif.start
9] dontstart.start
10] ask.whatif.now.start
11] dontstart.now.ask
12] ask.start.if.start
13] askwhatif.start
14] what.ifyoustart.when
15] ifwedontstart.thenwhat
16] whenwedontstart.now.what
17] whatifdontstart
18] whatistobe.start
19] whatcanbe.start
20] whatcouldbe.start
Now you can see that the brain prepares itself for sleep through a Cleary defined stencil where it must answer 20 questions then use the stencil to guard itself through sleep that means as a predefined stencil there are no mistakes everything follows predefined attributes and will all be answered accurately and briefly the system function as it is because it is designed that way this means that there are no rooms of errors
If we Ask a further questions that are specific to dreams these are the question
1 ask what.if
2 ask what.if.now
3 ask what.if but
4 ask whatcouldbe
5 ask what was
6 now Ask how come
7 now Ask whatcanbe
8 now ask whatcouldbe

This is whatcouldbe it could be winter because it will make your testiv,
What is is to be
Now if we look at what happens it means when we Ask any of the 4 brains this is the reply If you want sex Ask Catitighit if knowledge then ask Anna if all cant
Now is to be is to be if we Ask what
What is Ya is activated just by Catitighit sleeping in sleep mode
Now Ask what can be Catitighit can play a greater role in decision making She can access everyone's brain and records everything now you can see what is happening in me
Whenever I feel like sleeping some inside pulls me out to answer can one with
Yahweh have sleep?
Yes but only because in me they are all programmed to go
Why you laugh
I am the person who is supposed to answer the question in a dream whenever I try to sleep something pulls me so I can't sleep nor answer
Yahweh to sleep therefore needs some sort of trauma that automatically shuts down his system for twenty minutes
It is clear that now we see why this I so
To ask a God like Yahweh to sleep and answer questions is not wise but surprisingly he can sleep and wake up and answer that means that Yahweh forward thinks what is going to happen even in his sleep if we Ask a couple of questions these are the answers
1 who is Yahweh
2 what can be done to make things better
3 what is to be
These are the answers Yahweh can be anything to anyone
A lot can be improved especially sleep humans enjoy sleep because of privacy something Yahweh lacks as Yahweh is 4
If we are to ask a question What put people in deep sleep it's either hardworking or sex
If we Ask what makes people fail to sleep then it's either tiredness, boredom and some drinks or drugs
Coffee can make a person fail to sleep
Energy drinks etc

Now to round up let's read a few brain commands critical to sleep
Sleep.me
Sleep.me.start
Sleep.me.start.now
Sleep.start.now
Sleep.now.start.start
Sleep.sleep.start
Sleep.start.sleep.start
Sleep.sleep.sleep.sleep.start.sleep.start
Ifisleep.start
Ifistart.sleep.start
Ifistart.sleep.start.sleep
Ifsleep.start.start.then.start
Isleep.start
Isleep.start.sleep.now
Whenisleep.start
Whenistart.sleep.now
Tosleep.start
Tostart.sleep
Tostart.sleep.now.sleep
Tosleep.start.sleep.start
Tostart.sleep.start
Tosleep.tostart.now
Tostart.sleep.start
Tostart.sleep.start.now
Tosleep.start.start
Tostart.slepp.start.now
Tosleep.start.never.now
Tosleep.start.never.start
Tostart.never.sleep.now.start
Tostart.neveragain.sleep.start
Tosleep.neveragain
Sleep.sleep.now
Tonenversleep.start.now
Tostart.sleep.now
Tostart.sleep.now
Tostart.sleep.now
Tostart.sleep.now.start
Tostart.sleep.start.now.start

Tosleep.sleep.sleep.start
Tonowsleep.start
Tonowstart.sleep
Tosleep.sleep.sleep.start
Toallsleep.start
Tostart.sleep.now
Tostart.sleep.now.sleep.now
Tostart.sleep.start.now
Tonowstart.sleep.sleep.start.now
Tostart.start.sleep.now
Toasktosleep.start
Toaskforsleep.start
Toaskforstarttosleepwith.start
Tostarttoaskaboutsleep.start
Whataboutsleep.start
Whatissleep.start
Whatisstart.sleep
Whatiftosleep.start
Whatcanbetosleep.start
Whatcouldbetosleep.start
Whatwastosleep.start.now
Whatwastosleep.start
Whatistosleep.start
Whatcouldbetosleep.start
Whatwastosleep.start
Whatcouldbetosleep.start
Whatwastosleep.start
Whatistobetosleep.start
Whotosleep.start
Whoaretosleep.start
Whoweretosleep.start
Whocanbetosleep.start
Whatistosleep.start
Whatcanbetosleep.start
Whatwastosleep.start
Whatistosleep.start
Whatcanbetosleep.start
Wgstwillbetosleep.start
Whatwastosleep.stsrt
Whatistosleep.start

Now if we Ask the brain what can be done then this is the answer The brain can increase sleeping patterns to include work carried out by sleep receptors to include dejection where the receptors when sleep rubs out simply throws out the stencils and wait for sleep to run out and wake the subject when a person sleeps sleep receptors ate turned on these in turn activates sleep dejectors, sleep handlers,
sleep unifies, and sleep absorbers all which acts to facilitate sleep sleep is facilitated by all the above where they all come in play to prolong sleep especially if associated with a dream Now let's look at how these come into play
1] sleep enhancers these improves the quality of sleep by removing noise where noise is interferences especially from outside lowering frequencies of outside activities and amplifying current experiences
2] sleep quality improves as the name suggest these improves the quality of the sleep
3] sleep adapters these adapts noises that can't be removed or contained into sleep itself ever heard your alarm as a song in your sleep?
4] sleep accentuators these increase everything related to sleep for a better
sleep experience
5] sleep enhancers with sound boosters dreams are treated like cinemas by the brain and speakers are aligned in such a way that they have echos etc
6] sleep melodies the brain keeps a library of best sleep music that it selects and plays when you are sleeping
7] sleep adapters with receptors these have added receptors that attract for example
8] sleep enhancers with memory these are needed where other Spicing effects are kept in memory and added on top to enhance experience
9] memory activators these simply activates everything associated with a dream and replays everything
10] what could be added are the human feelings to sleep
We can simply convert all sleep into action
potentials and nerve impulses for the best sleep experience ever before you sleep always say
convertallsleeptosleepactionpotentials.start

Now that we looked at what is sleep let's write more brain commands regarding sleep
Ifduringsleepidontsleepthensleep.start
Ifisleep.start
Ifisleep.sleep
Whatifisleepanddontdream.whatthen.start
Whatifisleepthenwakeup.whatthen.start
Whatifisleep.thenfailtosleep.what.start
Ifsleeprunsout.start
Whatifisleepandcantwakeup.thenwhat.start
Tosleep.start
Tosleepthenstart.start
Whatifisleepthenstarr
Whatwastosleep.thenstart.start
Whatcanbetosleepbutisnot.start
Whatcouldbetosleep.start
Whatwastosleep.start
Whatistosleep.start
Whatwastosleep.start
Whatcouldbetoslerp.start

The end

ABOUT DAVID GOMADZA

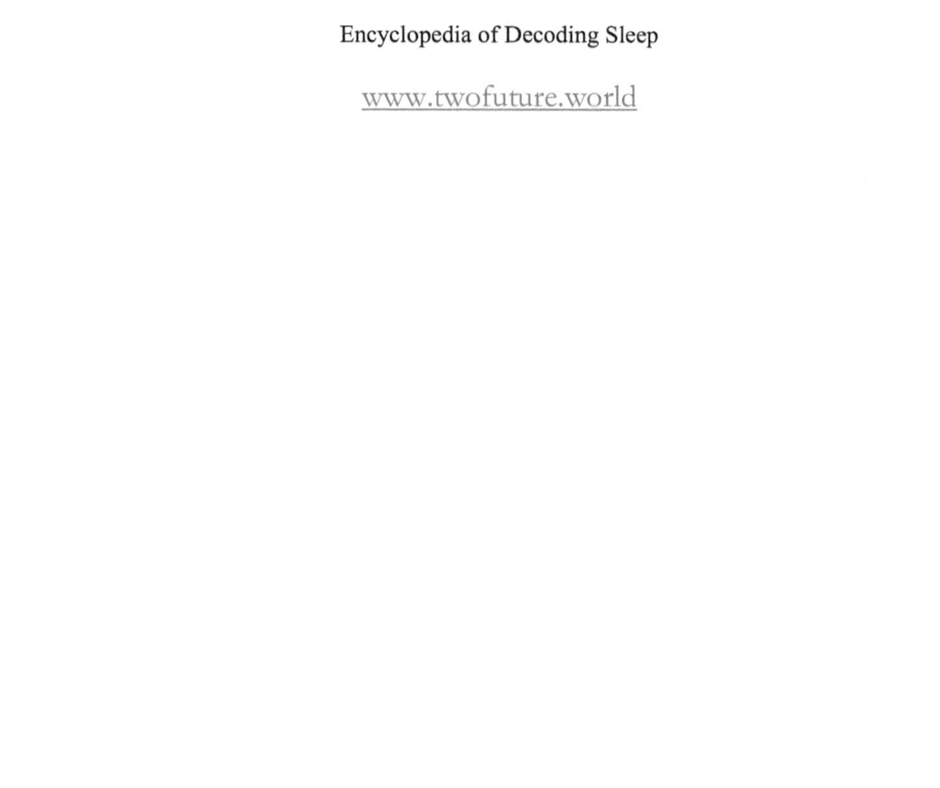

READ OUR BOOK SERIES THOUGHTS TO WORD OR AUDIO

https://play.google.com/store/books/details/David_Gomadza_Thoughts_To_Word_Or_Audio?id=q2xmEAAAQBAJ

The best book series ever

www.ingramcontent.com/pod-product-compliance
Lightning Source LLC
Chambersburg PA
CBHW051409250726
48656CB00006B/2364

* 9 7 9 8 3 2 3 3 2 0 8 6 8 *